中华人民共和国文化和旅游部 2022年文化和旅游发展统计公报

STATISTICAL COMMUNIQUÉ OF THE MINISTRY OF CULTURE AND TOURISM OF THE PEOPLE'S REPUBLIC OF CHINA ON CULTURAL AND TOURISM DEVELOPMENT IN 2022

中华人民共和国文化和旅游部 编

中国统计出版社
China Statistics Press

图书在版编目（CIP）数据

中华人民共和国文化和旅游部2022年文化和旅游发展统计公报 = Statistical Communiqu é of the Ministry of Culture and Tourism of the People' s Republic of China on Cultural and Tourism Development in 2022 : 汉英对照 / 中华人民共和国文化和旅游部编 . -- 北京 : 中国统计出版社 , 2023.8
ISBN 978-7-5230-0168-4

Ⅰ . ①中… Ⅱ . ①中… Ⅲ . ①文化发展－统计分析－公报－中国－ 2022 －汉、英②旅游业－统计分析－公报－中国－ 2022 －汉、英 Ⅳ . ① G12 ② F592

中国国家版本馆 CIP 数据核字 (2023) 第 138460 号

中华人民共和国文化和旅游部2022年文化和旅游发展统计公报

作　　者 / 中华人民共和国文化和旅游部
责任编辑 / 李　冲
执行编辑 / 张　怡
装帧设计 / 黄　晨
出版发行 / 中国统计出版社有限公司
通信地址 / 北京市西城区月坛南街57号
邮政编码 / 100826
办公地址 / 北京市丰台区西三环南路甲6号
网　　址 / http://www.zgtjcbs.com
电　　话 /（010）63376907（发行部）
印　　刷 / 北京画中画印刷有限公司
经　　销 / 新华书店
开　　本 / 880mm×1230mm　1/16
字　　数 / 52千字
印　　张 / 2.75
版　　别 / 2023年8月第1版
版　　次 / 2023年8月第1次印刷
定　　价 / 28.00元

目 录

CONTENTS

中华人民共和国文化和旅游部 2022 年文化和旅游发展统计公报[1]

2022 年，在以习近平同志为核心的党中央坚强领导下，全国文化和旅游系统深入学习贯彻习近平新时代中国特色社会主义思想，坚决贯彻落实党中央、国务院决策部署，紧扣迎接宣传贯彻党的二十大工作主线，坚持稳中求进、守正创新，围绕推进文化自信自强、建设社会主义文化强国，以满足人民精神文化需求和增强人民精神力量为着力点，推动文化和旅游各领域工作取得积极进展。出台《文化和旅游部关于建立健全"十四五"规划实施机制的意见》，制定"十四五"规划年度执行计划，推进年度重点任务和重大工程项目。统筹推进疫情防控和行业恢复发展，在更广范围、更深层次、更高水平上推动文化和旅游深度融合发展，激发新动能、形成新优势。坚持文化铸魂、文化赋能，以社会主义核心价值观为引领，推出一批优秀文艺作品，努力为人民群众提供更加丰富、更高质量的文化和旅游产品。推进实施国家文化数字化战略，推动文化和旅游数字化发展，促进文化和旅游新型业态与消费模式加快发展。加强文物和非物质文化遗产保护利用，中华文明探源工程取得突破，革命文物保护利用工程（2018—2022 年）圆满收官，非遗系统性保护水平不断提升，非遗在全社会的影响进一步扩大。协调推动长江、长城、长征、黄河、大运河国家文化公园建设。积极助力北京冬奥会、冬残奥会成功举行，深度拓展对外和对港澳台工作，不断提高国家文化软实力、增强中华文化影响力。

一、机构和人员

2022 年末，纳入统计范围的全国各类文化和旅游单位[2]31.40 万个，比上年末增加 0.19 万个。其中，各级文化和旅游部门所属单位 6.81 万个，增加 0.28 万个；从业人员[3]72.49 万人，增加 1.45 万人。

二、艺术创作演出

2022年，文化和旅游系统成功举办第十三届中国艺术节，81台优秀剧目完成158场线上线下精彩演出，展出美术、书法篆刻、摄影作品1000余件，超过3.5亿人次在线参与。组织实施新时代系列艺术创作工程，新时代现实题材创作工程、历史题材创作工程、全国舞台艺术优秀节目创作扶持计划、国家主题性美术创作项目等创作工程顺利推进实施，推出一批艺术精品。精心搭建展演展示平台，举办首届黄河流域戏曲演出季、2022年戏曲百戏（昆山）盛典等多项展演展示活动。坚持线上线下融合、演出演播并举，一批优秀剧目演播取得良好反响。持续推进文艺院团改革发展，推进美术馆、画院专业化建设，实施领军人才培养计划、京剧艺术表演人才提升计划、全国美术馆青年策展人扶持计划等。

2022年末，全国共有艺术表演团体[4]19739个，比上年末增加1369个；从业人员41.52万人，比上年末减少3.81万人。其中各级文化和旅游部门所属艺术表演团体1934个，占9.8%，从业人员10.71万人，占25.8%。

全年全国艺术表演团体共演出166.07万场，比上年下降28.6%；国内观众7.40亿人次，下降6.6%；演出收入80.95亿元，下降28.4%。积极克服疫情影响，大力发展线上演出和展播，全年全国艺术表演团体开展线上演出展播7.63万场次。

表1 2012-2022年全国艺术表演团体基本情况

年份	机构数（个）	从业人员（万人）	演出场次（万场）	国内演出观众人次（亿人次）	演出收入（亿元）
2012	7321	24.20	135.02	8.28	64.15
2013	8180	26.09	165.11	9.01	82.07
2014	8769	26.29	173.91	9.10	75.70
2015	10787	30.18	210.78	9.58	93.93
2016	12301	33.29	230.60	11.81	120.86
2017	15742	40.30	293.57	12.47	147.68
2018	17123	41.64	312.46	11.76	152.27
2019	17795	41.25	296.80	12.30	126.78
2020	17581	43.69	225.61	8.93	86.63
2021	18370	45.33	232.53	7.92	112.99
2022	19739	41.52	166.07	7.40	80.95

2022 年末，全国共有艺术表演场馆 3199 个，比上年末增加 106 个；观众坐席数 246.83 万个，减少 2.6%。其中文化和旅游部门所属艺术表演场馆 1052 个，比上年末减少 23 个，全年共开展艺术演出 4.35 万场次，比上年下降 13.5%；艺术演出观众人次 1424.16 万人次，下降 8.8%。

2022 年末，全国共有美术馆 718 个，比上年末增加 36 个，从业人员 6415 人，增加 166 人。全年共举办展览 7544 次，比上年增长 0.2%，参观人次 3588.92 万人次，增长 2.1%。

三、公共服务

2022 年，文化和旅游系统围绕《国家基本公共服务标准（2021 年版）》，推动公共服务效能有效提升。开展第七次全国县级以上公共图书馆评估定级，推广文化馆图书馆总分馆制建设模式，探索城乡新型公共文化空间建设。举办 2022 全国公共文化产品云上采购大会和区域性“文采会”。完成第一、二批 63 个国家公共文化服务体系示范区创新发展复核。推出 91 个具有区域影响力的“中国民间文化艺术之乡”典型范例。深入推进“春雨工程”“文化悦老”“文化筑梦”“文化助残”等志愿服务行动。创新开展群众文化活动，成功举办第十九届群星奖评奖活动，评出群星奖 30 个获奖作品，举办展演活动 1.8 万场；举办全国“村晚”示范展示活动 1.2 万场，参与群众达 1.18 亿人次。推动旅游公共服务稳步发展，推进旅游厕所建设和旅游厕所电子地图上线，旅游厕所电子地图手机 App 标注率达 96%。修订《旅游厕所质量要求与评定》国家标准。

（一）公共图书馆[5]

2022 年末，全国共有公共图书馆 3303 个，比上年末增加 88 个；从业人员 60740 人，增加 1439 人；其中具有高级职称人员 7850 人，占 12.9%；具有中级职称人员 19103 人，占 31.5%。

图 1 2012–2022 年全国公共图书馆人均资源情况

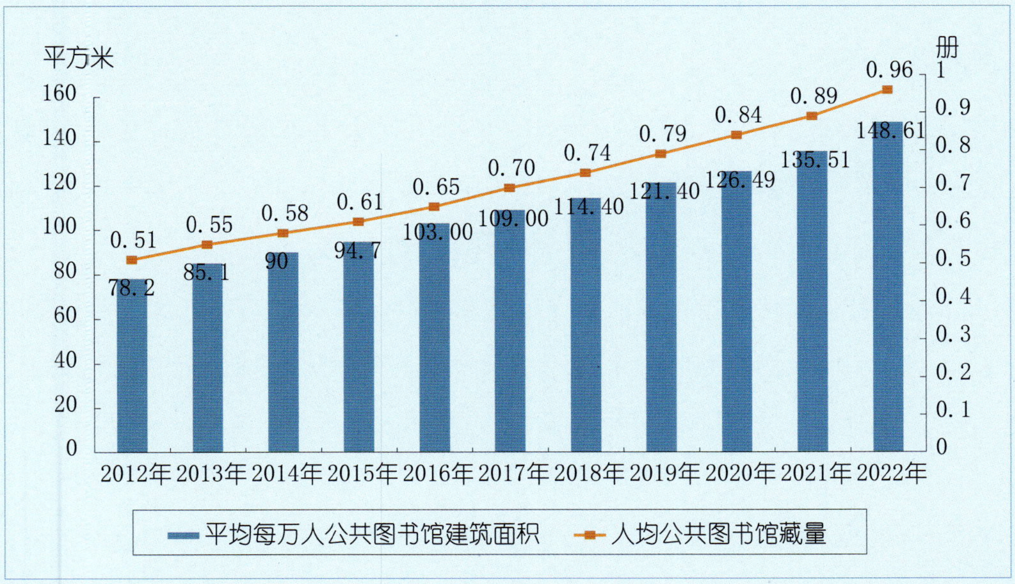

2022 年末，全国公共图书馆实际使用房屋建筑面积 2098 万平方米，比上年末增长 9.6%；全国公共图书馆总藏量[6]135959 万册，比上年末增长 7.8%；阅览室坐席数 155 万个，增长 15.4%。

2022 年末，全国平均每万人公共图书馆建筑面积 148.61 平方米，比上年末增加 13.1 平方米，全国人均图书藏量 0.96 册，增加 0.07 册；全年全国人均购书费 1.67 元，增加 0.1 元。

全国公共图书馆累计发放借书证 12229 万个；总流通人次[7]78970 万，比上年增长 5.8%；书刊文献外借 60719 万册次，增长 3.4%；外借人次 24894 万，增长 4.6%。全年共为读者举办各种活动 21.23 万次，比上年增长 4.8%；参加人次 13495 万，增长 13.5%。推动全国智慧图书馆体系建设，采取线上线下相结合的方式，为读者提供优质服务。

图 2 2012-2022 年全国公共图书馆总流通人次及书刊外借册次

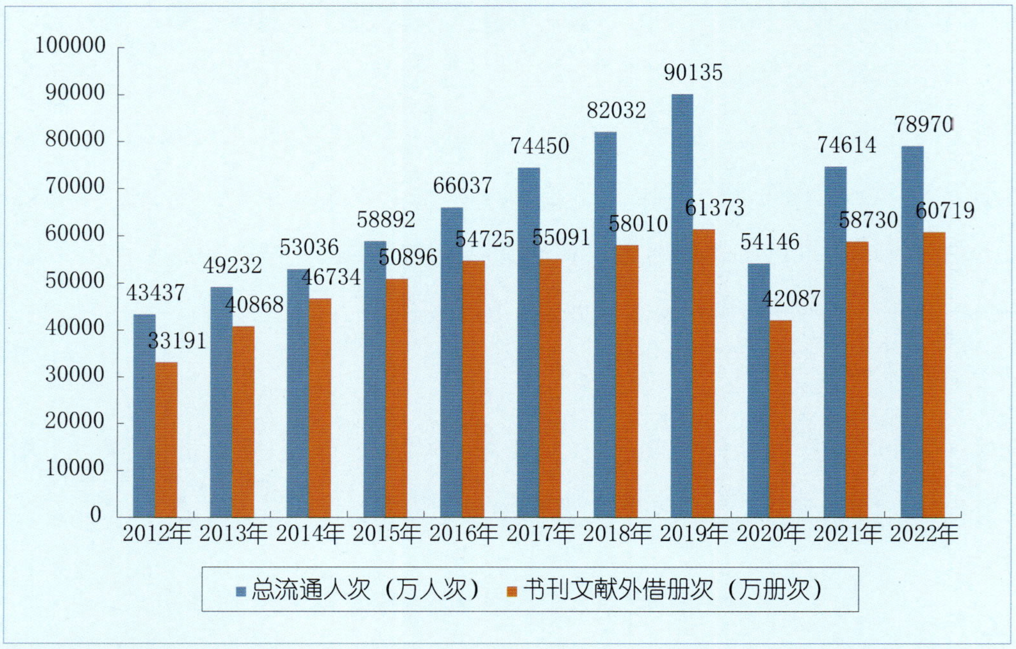

（二）群众文化机构[8]

2022 年末，全国共有群众文化机构 45623 个，比上年末增加 2092 个。其中乡镇综合文化站 33932 个，增加 1408 个。年末全国群众文化机构从业人员 195826 人，比上年末增加 5819 人。其中具有高级职称的人员 7868 人，占 4.0%；具有中级职称人员 18262 人，占 9.3%。

2022 年末，全国群众文化机构实际使用房屋建筑面积 5298 万平方米，比上年末增长 6.5%；业务用房面积 3668 万平方米，增长 3.7%。年末全国平均每万人群众文化设施建筑面积 375.25 平方米，增长 6.6%。

图 3 2012-2022 年全国平均每万人群众文化设施建筑面积

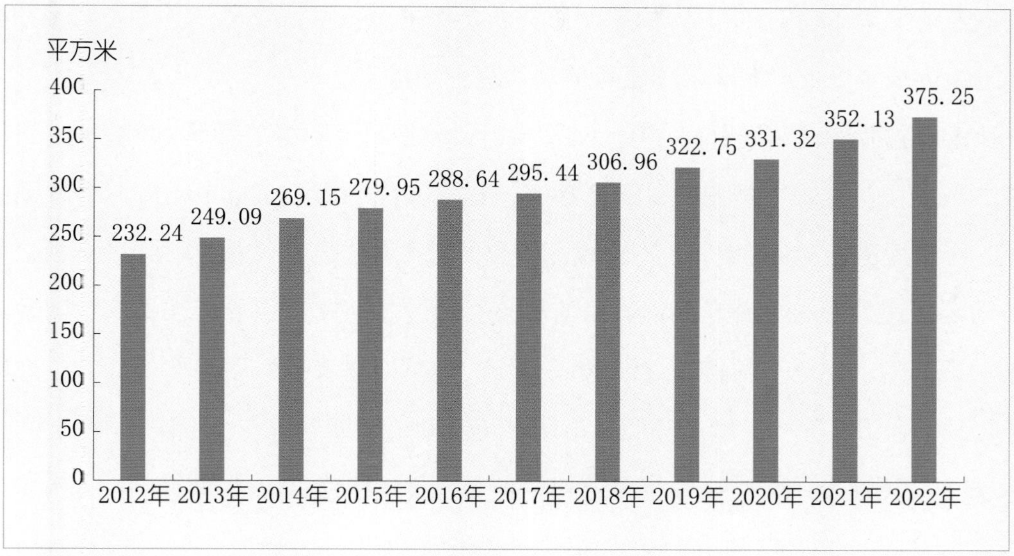

全年全国群众文化机构共组织开展各类文化活动[9]270.73 万场次，比上年增长 7.4%；服务人次 95922 万人次，增长 15.2%。全年全国群众文化机构组织开展线上群众文化活动 280.96 万次。

2022 年末，全国群众文化机构共有馆办文艺团体[10]9322 个，演出 10.32 万场，观众 5442 万人次。由文化馆（站）指导的群众业余文艺团体 46.36 万个。

表 2 2022 年全国群众文化机构活动开展情况

项 目	总量		比上年增长（%）	
	活动次数（次）	服务人次（万人次）	活动次数	服务人次
各项活动总计	**2707286**	**95922**	**7.4**	**15.2**
其中：文艺活动	1607329	68474	15.5	10.2
训练班	879961	6811	-4.4	11.3
展览	177506	19872	6.0	39.4
公益性讲座	42490	762	1.3	-0.8

四、市场管理和综合执法

2022 年，文化和旅游系统科学精准做好行业疫情防控工作。结合疫情形势变化，不断优化跨省旅游管理政策，根据“二十条优化措施”“新十条优化措施”，及时调整活动、场所、人员等管理措施，及时对公共图书馆和文化馆（站）、旅游景区、旅行社、互联网上网服务营业场所、娱乐场所、剧院等演出场所、剧本娱乐经营场所、社会艺术水平考级现场考级活动等 8 项行业防控指南进行修订。联合有关部门，从减税降费、稳岗拓岗、社保缓缴、金融支持、房租减免等方面推出一系列针对性举措，支持文化和旅游行业恢复发展。将旅游服务质量保证金暂退比例提高至 100%，暂退、缓交保证金 96 亿元，批复同意海南等 14 省（市）开展旅游服务质量保证金改革试点工作。举办文化和旅游企业服务月活动，组织各地集中推出 800 余项服务活动和惠企举措。

文化和旅游部持续优化市场营商环境，全面实行行政许可事项清单管理，持续推进“一网通办”，开展“延期办”工作，推进“好差评”制度落实，建成文化和旅游市场电子证照管理系统。修订部门规章 2 部、行政规范性文件 30 个，不断规范演出经纪人员、营业性演出、娱乐场所、乡村民宿、剧本娱乐活动等管理。发布导游专业素养研培要点、旅游景区文明引导工作指南，印发星级饭店从业人员三年培训计划，完成全国特级导游考评工作。规范网络直播、明星广告代言，规范网络主播行为。做好元旦、春节、五一、国庆等假日市场以及汛期、暑期旅游安全工作。

2022 年末，全国通过统计直报系统报送的各类文化市场经营单位[11] 共计 20.28 万家，从业人员 134.00 万人，营业收入 14106.44 亿元，营业利润 2349.97 亿元。

2022 年末，全国共有旅行社 32603 家。旅行社填报数据显示，全年全国旅行社营业收入 1601.56 亿元，营业利润亏损 68.87 亿元。

2022 年末，全国共有星级饭店 8365 家，其中 7337 家的经营数据通过省级文化和旅游部门审核。填报数据显示，全年全国星级饭店营业收入 1177.68 亿元，平均房价 318.48 元，平均出租率 38.35%。

2022 年，文化市场综合执法体制机制进一步完善，推动 3 万余名执法人员统一配发制式服装和标志，完善执法人员资格证件管理，29 个省（区、市）印发执法事项指导目录、20 个省（区、市）编制行政处罚裁量基准。扎实开展迎接党的二十大文化和旅游市场执法保障行动，做好北京冬奥会期间执法监管。加强文娱领域综合治理，清理涉劣迹艺人文化产品，开展净化艺术品市场环境专项行动。持续推进打击治理跨境赌博旅游管控工作，深入推进未经许可经营旅行社业务、“不合理低价游”等专项整治行动。组织 3 轮暗访评估，访查 29 个省（区、市）1200 余家经营单位。常态化开展网络监测，清查问题线索 5.4 万条。全面完成电话热线整合任务，高效处置文化和旅游市场举报投诉信息 3.1 万条。全年共出动执法人员 931 万人次，检查各类场所 333 万家次，办结案件 3.6 万件。举办以案施训、师资培训等线上线下培训，覆盖执法人员 1.3 万人次。

五、资源开发和利用

2022 年，文化和旅游部加强规划和制度引领，制定长江国家文化公园建设实施方案和保护规划，编制实施京张体育文化旅游带、巴蜀文化旅游走廊、杭黄自然生态和文化旅游廊道等规划，完善世界级旅游景区度假区建设方案，发布新版《旅游度假区等级划分》国家标准，印发《国民旅游休闲发展纲要（2022—2030 年）》，出台十四部门关于露营旅游休闲的指导意见。不断丰富优质旅游产品供给，23 个省（区、市）开展旅游资源普查，新评定 12 家国家 5A 级旅游景区、15 家国家级旅游度假区、54 家国家级旅游休闲街区，推出首批 53 家国家工业旅游示范基地、12 家国家级滑雪旅游度假地、14 家体育旅游示范基地。提升乡村旅游发展品质，推出第四批 298 个全国乡村旅游重点村镇，发布“乡村四时好风光”系列主题线路 369 条。广西大寨村和重庆荆竹村成功入选联合国世界旅游组织“最佳旅游乡村”名单。推出 8 条长城主题国家级旅游线路。创新旅游宣传推广，推出《山水间的家》《正大综艺—不看不知道，山河真美妙》节目。开展“美丽中国 美好生活”国内旅游推广活动，实施“跟着季节游中国”“城市巡游记”专项推广，开展第二届全国旅游公益广告作品遴选展播。发布《智慧旅游场景应用指南（试行）》，开展智慧旅游“上云用数赋智”行动。开展红色旅游融合发展试点建设工作，举办全国大学生红色旅游创意策划大赛、红色讲解员进校园活动达 1.1 万余场次，覆盖大中小学生 4700 万人次。

2022 年末，全国共有 A 级景区 14917 个，直接从业人员 147 万人，全年接待总人数 26.3 亿人次，实现旅游收入 1818.5 亿元。

2022 年，国内旅游总人次 25.30 亿，同比下降 22.1%。国内旅游收入（旅游总消费）2.04 万亿元，同比下降 30.0%。

图 4 2012-2022 年国内旅游发展情况

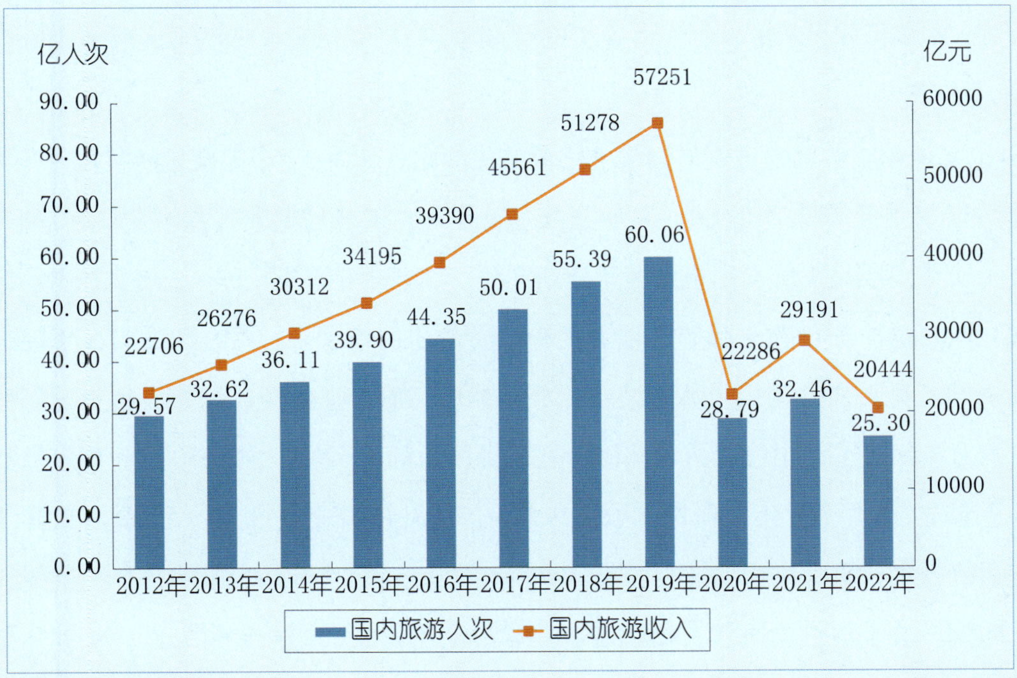

六、产业与科技

2022 年，文化和旅游部印发《关于推动文化产业赋能乡村振兴的意见》，启动文化产业赋能乡村振兴试点工作。实施“文化产业园区携行计划”，推动区域文化产业协同发展。公布第二批 123 个国家级夜间文化和旅游消费集聚区名单，实施“百城百区”文化和旅游消费助企惠民行动计划。推进数字文化产业快速发展，推动 5G、超高清等技术广泛应用，推动国有文艺院团开发《抗战中的文艺》线上演播、《只此青绿》数字艺术品等项目。联合印发《虚拟现实与行业应用融合发展行动计划》，培育线上演播、沉浸式体验等新型业态。联合商务部印发《关于开展新一批国家对外文化贸易基地申报工作的通知》，部署开展新一批国家对外文化贸易基地申报工作。在江西景德镇组织举办“多彩中国　佳节好物”文化和旅游贸易促进活动（陶瓷文创专题）。联合日本经济产业省、韩国文化体育观光部举办第 15 届中日韩文化产业论坛，支持举办东亚电竞交流活动。联合印发《关于推进对外文化贸易高质量发展的意见》，修订文化产品和服务进出口统计目录、鼓励外商投资产业目录等，举办第十八届中国（深圳）国际文化产业博览交易会。建立产业项目协调推进机制，会同中国人民银行推出文化和旅游企业“白名单”等政策措施，争取基础设施政策性开发性贷款支持，推送 30 余家文化和旅游骨干企业、171 个重点项目。推动文化和旅游领域纳入设备购置和更新改造新增贷款贴息政策支持范围，1237 个项目纳入备选名单，项目总投资 2461 亿元。完成 2021 年度文化产业和旅游产业工作拟激励地市推荐工作，由我部推荐的 10 个地市纳入国务院办公厅激励地市名单。

根据国家统计局统计，2022 年全国规模以上文化及相关产业企业实现营业收入 121805 亿元，比上年增长 0.9%。其中，文化新业态特征较为明显的 16 个行业小类实现营业收入 43860 亿元，比上年增长 5.3%。

2022 年，文化和旅游部推进实施国家文化数字化战略，认定 12 个国家旅游科技示范园区，资助 14 个文化和旅游部重点实验室研究项目，推进实施文化和旅游领域国家重点研发计划，评定发布“长安十二时辰＋大唐不夜城”唐文化全景展示创新实践、“建筑可阅读”——上海文旅融合创新实践、舞蹈诗剧《只此青绿》的创新实践等三项文化和旅游最佳创新成果。联合印发《关于促进团体标准规范优质发展的意见》。推动出台舞台装备、旅游厕所、旅游度假区、旅游民宿等国家标准 4 项、立项 1 项，发布演出安全、出境旅游领队服务规范等行业标准 7 项、立项 30 项。国家社科基金艺术学项目重大项目立项 18 个、年度项目立项 219 个，部级社科研究项目立项 51 项。实施“2022 年度文化和旅游系统青年科研人才扶持计划”项目 36 个。推进文化和旅游行业智库体系建设。加强高校共建工作。印发《关于促进新时代文化艺术职业教育高质量发展的指导意见》。实施全国文化艺术职业教育和旅游职业教育“提质培优”行动计划，入选 115 个项目。举办第七届中国京剧优秀青年演员研究生班，招生 54 人。实施西藏、新疆基层文化人才共建培养项目，招生 24 人（本科）。

七、文化遗产保护利用

2022 年，推动完善顶层设计，高规格召开全国文物工作会议，确定“保护第一、加强管理、挖掘价值、有效利用、让文物活起来”的新时代文物工作方针。推动出台《关于让文物活起来扩大中华文化国际影响力的意见》，修订实施《水下文物保护管理条例》。出台《“十四五”考古工作专项规划》，中华文明探源工程取得新突破。推进夏文化、高句丽等 18 项“考古中国”重大项目，发布旧石器考古与人类起源研究、殷墟考古与甲骨文研究等 17 项重要成果。加强基本建设考古勘探管理，23 个省市落实“先考古、后出让”。组织建设国家重点区域考古标本库房。实施“全国考古人才振兴计划”。评定第四批国家考古遗址公园。推动不可移动文物保护管理纳入全国国土空间规划纲要。推动流失文物追索返还工作常态化，29 件流失文物艺术品回归祖国，启动流失海外文物数字复原工程。革命文物保护利用工程（2018—2022 年）圆满收官，16 个省份完成第二批革命文物名录核定公布。推动文物活化利用。举办 2022 年文化和自然遗产日文物保护主题宣传活动、“5 · 18 国际博物馆日”中国主会场活动，出台《关于鼓励和支持社会力量参与文物建筑保护利用的意见》，《中国考古大会》《中国国宝大会》等节目反响良好。

2022 年末，全国共有各类文物机构 11340 个，比上年末增加 795 个，其中，文物保护管理机构 2663 个，占 23.5%；文物系统管理的国有博物馆[12]3782 个，占 33.4%。年末全国文物机构从业人员 19.03 万人，比上年末增加 0.88 万人。其中高级职称 12757 人，占 6.7%；中级职称 24129 人，占 12.7%。

图 5 2012-2022 年全国文物机构及从业人员情况

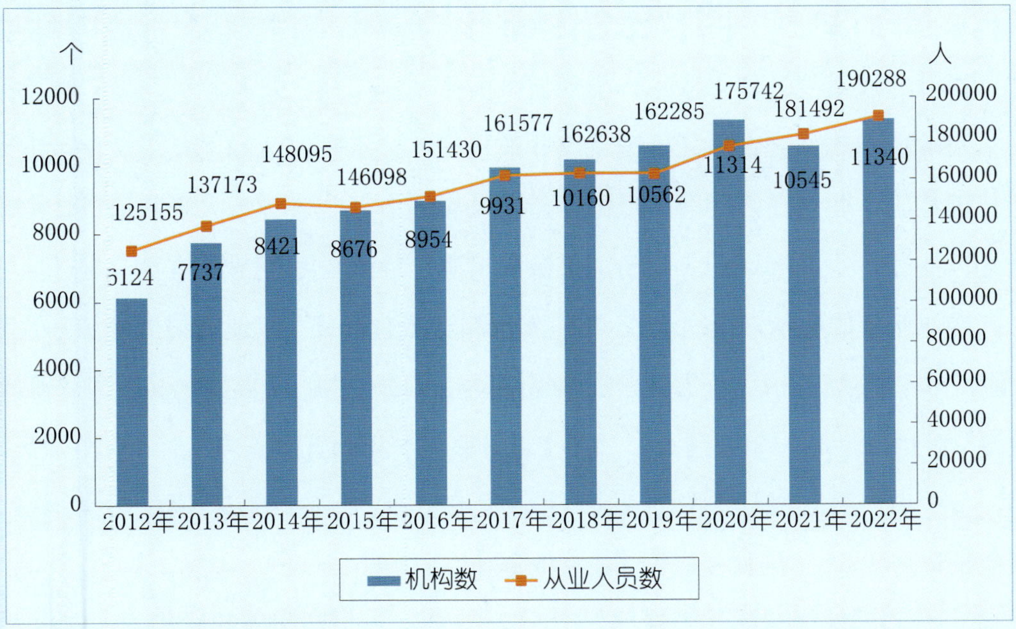

2022 年末，全国文物机构藏品 5630.43 万件，其中，博物馆文物藏品 4691.61 万件/套，占文物藏品总量的 83.3%。

2022 年，全国各类文物机构共举办陈列展览 32357 个，比上年减少 848 个。其中，基本陈列[13]17399 个，减少 198 个；临时展览[14]14958 个，减少 650 个。接待观众 63973 万人次，比上年减少 24.4%，其中未成年人 16004 万人次，减少 19.6%，占参观总人数的 25.0%。文物系统管理的国有博物馆接待观众 45647 万人次，比上年减少 22.8%。

图 6 2012-2022 年全国文物机构接待观众人次及未成年人观众人次

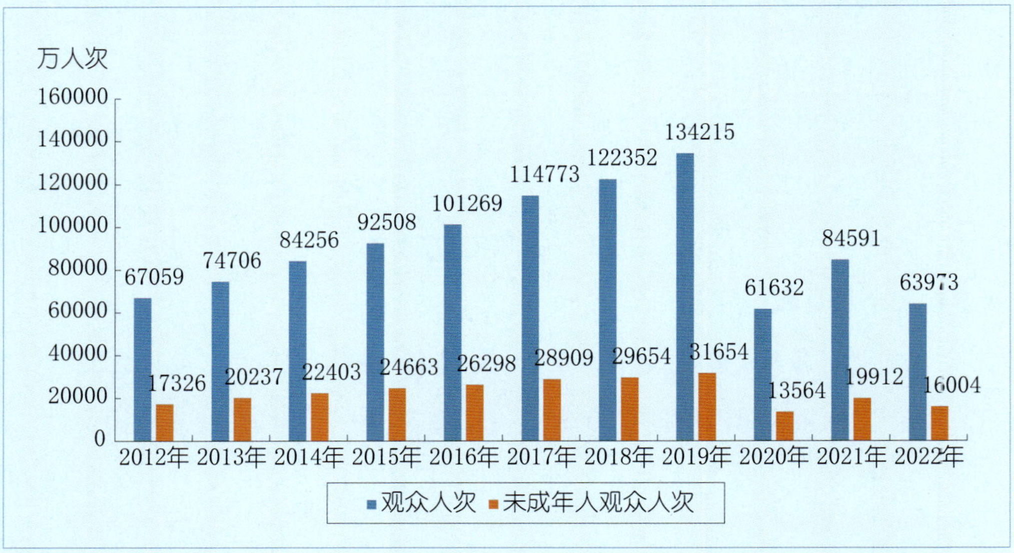

2022 年，文化和旅游部修订《国家非物质文化遗产保护资金管理办法》，印发《关于推动传统工艺高质量传承发展的通知》，研究制定国家级非遗代表性项目管理办法、非遗与旅游融合发展的通知等文件。提升非遗系统性保护水平，推动"中国传统制茶技艺及其相关习俗"成功列入联合国教科文组织人类非遗代表作名录。开展国家级非遗代表性传承人评估和国家级文化生态保护实验区验收工作。持续推进"非遗在社区"试点工作。深入实施中国非遗传承人研修培训计划、中国传统工艺振兴计划、曲艺传承发展计划。启动国家级非遗生产性保护示范基地推荐。推进非遗学科专业建设。大力开展非遗宣传展示，组织 2022 年"文化和自然遗产日"非遗宣传展示活动，举办"云游非遗·影像展""非遗购物节"等，全国共开展非遗活动达 6200 多项。举办第七届中国非遗博览会、"新疆是个好地方"对口援疆 19 省市非遗展、"文化进万家——视频直播家乡年""茶和天下 共享非遗"等主题活动。与中央广播电视总台联合摄制《非遗里的中国》。各地累计建设非遗工坊 2500 余家，覆盖 450 余个脱贫县和 85 个国家乡村振兴重点帮扶县。

2022 年末，全国国家级非遗代表性项目 1557 项，共有在世国家级非遗代表性传承人 2433 名。

列入联合国教科文组织人类非物质文化遗产代表作名录（名册）项目 43 个，位居世界第一。

全国共有非物质文化遗产保护机构 2425 个，从业人员 17716 人。全年全国各类非物质文化遗产保护机构举办演出 57762 场，比上年下降 3.3%；举办民俗活动 13664 次，增长 4.2%；举办展览 18107 场，与去年基本持平。

八、文化和旅游对外及对港澳台交流

2022 年，文化和旅游部坚持围绕中心、服务大局，积极助力北京冬奥会、冬残奥会成功举办，举办欢迎北京冬奥会国际贵宾文艺演出、“欢乐春节”庙会、“相约北京”奥林匹克文化节暨“相约北京”国际艺术节、“欢乐冰雪旅游季”品牌推广等活动，发布“筑梦冰雪 相伴冬奥”全国冰雪旅游精品线路、国家级滑雪旅游度假地等，精心组织主题文化宣传。

实施共建“文化丝路”三年行动计划。推动世界旅游联盟总部落户杭州，举办中国国际旅游交易会、“发现中国之旅”“东亚文化之都”等活动。联动开展“中国影像节”全球展映活动、“海外中国旅游文化周”“非遗减贫展”。组织举办 2022 年“欢乐春节”系列活动，策划“经典文化”“魅力冰雪”“乐享生活”三个版块 14 个文化和旅游精品线上项目，境外浏览量超过 6261 万人次。

召开中俄文化和旅游部长级会议，举办中俄文化大集等活动。参与爱丁堡国际文化峰会、第 59 届威尼斯国际艺术双年展。组织参加东盟－中日韩、中国－东盟、中日韩等合作机制，召开文化和旅游部长会。实施亚洲旅游促进计划。与阿根廷等 12 个亚非拉国家举办建交庆祝活动，参与第 14 届达喀尔非洲当代艺术双年展、第 14 届哈瓦那双年展，办好非洲国家人力资源培训班。举办金砖国家文化部长会议和旅游部长会议。参加联合国教科文组织世界文化政策与可持续发展大会、联合国世界旅游组织 2022 世界旅游合作与发展大会。

文化和旅游部坚持培根铸魂，深化对港澳台工作。举办香港故宫文化博物馆开幕典礼，支持香港举办“亚洲文化合作论坛”。开展庆祝香港回归 25 周年文化遗产系列活动。支持澳门举办中国（澳门）创意产业大会、澳门旅游博览会。推动港澳 18 个项目获得国家艺术基金资助。举办“情系三江源 · 大美青海情”联谊活动、两岸非物质文化遗产月等活动。参加台北夏季旅展、高雄旅展。举办“港澳大学生文化实践”“港澳青少年内地云游学”“情系青春”等活动。

截至 2022 年末，在全球设有 45 家海外中国文化中心，20 家驻外旅游办事处。此外，在香港设有亚洲旅游交流中心，在台湾设有海峡两岸旅游交流协会台北办事处、高雄办事分处。

九、资金投入

2022 年，稳步推进重大文化工程项目建设，中国工艺美术馆（中国非物质文化遗产馆）、中央歌剧院剧场工程竣工运营，故宫博物院北院区、中央芭蕾舞团业务用房项目启动施工，“十四五”

文化保护传承利用工程顺利推进。

图7 2012-2022年全国人均文化和旅游事业费及增速情况

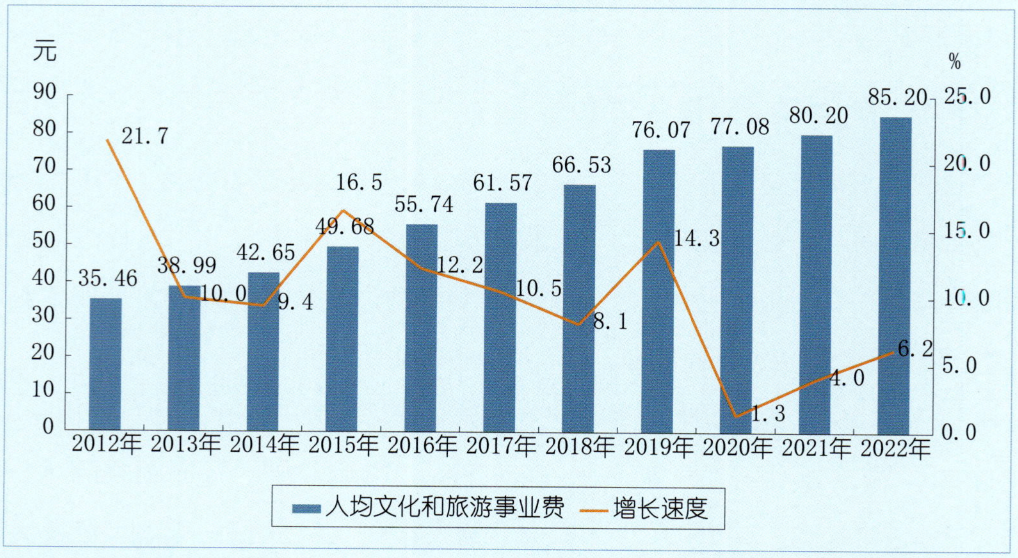

表3 全国文化和旅游事业费按城乡和区域分布情况

项目		1995	2000	2005	2010	2015	2020	2021	2022
总量(亿元)	全国	33.4	63.2	133.8	323.1	686.0	1088.3	1132.9	1202.9
	#县以上	24.4	46.3	98.1	206.7	352.8	501.0	506.4	544.3
	县及县以下	9.0	16.9	35.7	116.4	330.1	587.3	626.5	658.6
	#东部地区	13.4	28.9	64.4	143.4	287.9	491.6	526.4	542.5
	中部地区	9.5	15.1	30.6	78.7	164.3	269.8	283.4	302.6
	西部地区	8.3	13.7	27.6	85.8	193.9	301.6	292.6	328.1
所占比重(%)	全国	100	100	100	100	100	100	100	100
	#县以上	73.2	73.4	73.3	64.0	51.7	46.0	44.7	45.2
	县及县以下	26.8	26.7	26.7	36.0	48.3	54.0	55.3	54.8
	#东部地区	40.2	45.7	48.1	44.4	42.1	45.1	46.5	45.1
	中部地区	28.6	23.8	22.9	24.3	24.1	24.8	25.0	25.2
	西部地区	24.9	21.7	20.6	26.6	28.4	27.7	25.8	27.3

2022 年，全国文化和旅游事业费[15]1202.89 亿元，比上年增加 70.01 亿元，增长 6.2%；全国人均文化和旅游事业费 85.20 元，比上年增加 5 元，增长 6.2%。文化和旅游事业费占财政总支出的比重为 0.46%，与去年基本持平。

全国文化和旅游事业费中，县以上文化和旅游事业费 544.29 亿元，占 45.2%，比重比上年提高 0.5 个百分点；县及县以下文化和旅游事业费 658.61 亿元，占 54.8%，比重下降了 0.5 个百分点。东部地区[15]文化和旅游事业费 542.53 亿元，占 45.1%，比重下降了 1.4 个百分点。中部地区文化和旅游事业费 302.56 亿元，占 25.2%，比重提高了 0.2 个百分点。西部地区文化和旅游事业费 328.09 亿元，占 27.3%，比重提高了 1.5 个百分点。

注释：

[1] 本公报中各项数据为初步统计数据。各项统计数据均未包括香港特别行政区、澳门特别行政区和台湾省。部分数据因四舍五入的原因，存在着与分项合计不等的情况。

[2] 文化和旅游单位是指全国各级文化和旅游部门主办的或实行行业管理的文化机构，不含各级新闻出版、广播影视等部门主办或管理的机构。根据现行的统计制度，各级文化和旅游部门主办单位（如公共图书馆、文化馆、文化站、博物馆、公有制艺术表演团体、公有制艺术表演场馆等）全部纳入统计范围，实行行业管理的文化和旅游单位中，包括娱乐场所和互联网上网服务营业场所、非公有制艺术表演团体、非公有制艺术表演场馆、经营性互联网文化单位、艺术品经营机构和演出经纪机构和 A 级景区、星级饭店和旅行社数据。

[3] 从业人员是指各级文化和旅游部门主办或实行行业管理的机构中工作并取得劳动报酬的人员。

[4] 艺术表演团体指由文化和旅游部门主办或实行行业管理（经文化和旅游行政部门审批并领取营业性演出许可证），专门从事表演艺术等活动的各类专业艺术表演团体。

[5] 公共图书馆是指由各级文化和旅游部门主办的、面向社会公众开放并提供科学、文化等各种知识普及教育的机构。

[6] 公共图书馆总藏量指已编目的古籍、图书、期刊和报纸的合订本、手册、手稿，以及缩微制品、录像带、录音带、光盘等视听文献资料数量之和，不包括电子图书。

[7] 公共图书馆总流通人次是指本年度内到图书馆场馆接受图书馆服务的总人次，包括借阅书刊、咨询问题，以及参加各类读者活动等。

[8] 群众文化机构是指各级文化和旅游部门主办的开展群众文化活动的场所，主要包括文化馆（含综合性文化中心、群众艺术馆）、文化站。

[9] 群众文化机构组织开展活动是指组织文艺活动、举办训练班、举办展览和组织公益性讲座总和。

[10] 群众文化机构馆办文艺团体指由本馆人员组成的为群众提供文艺演出的演出团队。

[11] 文化市场经营单位指经审批或备案并领取相关许可或备案文件的、从事文化经营和文化服务活动的机构。按照现行统计制度，文化市场经营单位统计范围包括娱乐场所和互联网上网服务营业场所、非公有制艺术表演团体、非公有制艺术表演场馆、经营性互联网文化单位、艺术品经营机构和演出经纪机构。

[12] 博物馆指为了研究、教育、欣赏的目的，收藏、保护、展示人类活动和自然环境的见证物，向公众开放，非营利性、永久性社会服务机构，包括以博物馆（院）、纪念馆（舍）、科技馆、陈列馆等专有名称开展活动的单位。

[13] 基本陈列指在本馆布置陈列、地点固定、时间较长的展出。

[14] 临时展览指在本机构内设置，由本馆设计布陈，形式比较多样的展出。

[15] 文化和旅游事业费是指区域内各级财政对文化和旅游系统主办单位的经费投入总和。根据现行统计口径，文化和旅游事业费不包括各级文化和旅游行政部门的行政运行经费。

[16] 东部地区包括北京、天津、辽宁、上海、江苏、浙江、福建、山东、广东；中部地区包括河北、山西、吉林、黑龙江、安徽、江西、河南、湖北、湖南、海南；西部地区包括内蒙古、广西、重庆、四川、贵州、云南、西藏、陕西、甘肃、青海、宁夏、新疆。

Statistical Communiqué of the Ministry of Culture and Tourism of the People's Republic of China on Cultural and Tourism Development in 2022[1]

In 2022, under the firm leadership of the Central Committee of the Communist Party of China with Comrade Xi Jinping at its core, China's cultural and tourism administrations fully implemented Xi Jinping Thought on Socialism with Chinese Characteristics for A New Era and the decisions and plans of the Central Committee of the Communist Party of China and the State Council, acted on the general principle of pursuing progress while ensuring stability, and upheld fundamental principles and break new ground. With the focus on put into practice the spirit of 20th CPC National Congress, and aiming to develop China into a nation with a strong socialist culture and cultural confidence, and to meet the intellectual and cultural needs of our people, and strengthen culture as their source of inspiration, they worked hard to ensure that steady progresses were made in China's cultural and tourism undertakings. For instance, the Ministry published its opinions on build and improve the implementation mechanism of the 14th Five Year Plan, and formulated an annual executive program based on the 14th Five Year Plan, which included a series of key tasks and major projects. With equal priority attached to Covid-19 pandemic prevention and control, the Ministry focused on ushering in the recovery of cultural and tourism sectors, and made strong efforts to find new energy and competitive edges in such sectors through forging stronger and more extensive synergy between culture and tourism. Giving full play to the role of culture in shaping minds and empower individual development, the Ministry introduced a wide range of outstanding performing arts productions that celebrated the socialist core values and high-quality travel products to enrich people's lives. To implement the national strategy of digitizing cultural content, the Ministry promoted the use of digital technology in cultural and tourism sectors, and facilitated the fast development of new business forms and consumers' spending patterns in these sectors. Stronger measures were taken to protect and manage cultural heritage and intangible cultural heritage (ICH), new breakthroughs were made in the project aimed at tracing the origins of Chinese civilization, the project to preserve and harness revolutionary heritage for social benefits (2018-2022) was completed with satisfying results, ICH safeguarding measures were more systematic and efficient, and public awareness of ICH was further raised. The Ministry coordinated and supported the development of cultural parks with the themes of the Great Wall, the Long March, the Yellow River and the Grand Canal, and made strong contribution to the success of the Beijing Winter Olympic Games and Winter Paralympics. With new achievements made in the Ministry's work to promote extensive and in-depth international cultural cooperation and cultural bonding with Hong Kong, Macao and Taiwan, China's cultural soft power and the international influence of Chinese culture have increased steadily.

I. Organization and Headcount

314,000 national cultural and tourism units[2] were brought into the statistical range by the end of 2022, 1,900 more than the number of the previous year. Among them, 68,100 were affiliated to cultural and tourism authorities at different levels, 2,800 more than that of the previous year. They hired 724,900 employees[3], 14,500 more than those of the previous year.

II. Performing Arts

In 2022, the China's cultural and tourism administrations successfully held the 13th China Arts Festival, which presented 158 on-site and online performances of 81 outstanding productions, as well as over 1,000 artworks including paintings, caligraphy and seal carving works. The Festival attracted over 350 million visitor attendances online. The Ministry also initiated a series of new new-era-themed art projects, and continued to organize projects including the projects of art production based on true stories and historic events, the national support program for outstanding performing arts shows, and the national fine arts creation project focusing on important occasions. We put great efforts in building platforms for art presentations, as we organized the first Yellow River xiqu performing arts season and the 2022 xiqu gala in Kunshan city, Jiangsu Province. We gave equal priority to on-site and online performances, and the audience welcomed the broadcasting of outstanding production online. The reform and development of art troupes were further advanced, more efforts were put into capacity building of art museums and fine arts museums, and talent development programs such as leading artists program, Peking opera actors capacity building program and the national supporting program for young curators in art museums.

By the end of the year, the number of art performance troupes[4] reached 19,739, an increase of 1,369 over the end of the previous year; that of the professionals reached 415,200 with a decrease of 38,100. Of them, the number of art performance troupes managed by cultural and tourism departments at all levels reached 1,934, accounting for 9.8% of the total with 107,100 professionals, which was 25.8% of the total.

In 2022, all arts troupes in China presented 1.6607 million performances, a decrease of 28.6% over the previous year; the domestic audiences reached 740 million, down by 6.6%. The total performing arts box office was 8.095 billion yuan, down by 28.4%. To respond to the pandemic, we made much efforts to support online shows and live broadcasting. Throughout the year, there were 76,300 performances delivered online by art troupes all over China.

By the end of the year, the number of venues of the performing arts amounted to 3,199, 106 more than those of the previous year, with 2,468,300 seats, down by 2.6%. 43,500 art performances were held throughout the year, down by 13.5% over the previous year; the audience reached 14.2416 million, a decrease of 8.8%. Among the venues, 1,052 were affiliated to the cultural and tourism departments, down by 23 compared to that of previous year.

By the end of 2022, there were 718 art museums in China, 36 more than those of the previous year, with 6,415 employees, 166 more than the previous year. 7,544 exhibitions were presented by these museums year-round, up by 0.2%, attracting 35.8892 million visitor attendances, up by 2.1% over the number of the previous year.

Table 1: General information of art troupes nationwide in 2012-2022

Year	Number of institutions (unit)	Number of employees (ten thousand)	Number of shows (ten thousand)	Number of domestic audience attendances (one hundred million person-time)	Shows' box office (one hundred million yuan)
2012	7321	24.20	135.02	8.28	64.15
2013	8180	26.09	165.11	9.01	82.07
2014	8769	26.29	173.91	9.10	75.70
2015	10787	30.18	210.78	9.58	93.93
2016	12301	33.29	230.60	11.81	120.86
2017	15742	40.30	293.57	12.47	147.68
2018	17123	41.64	312.46	11.76	152.27
2019	17795	41.25	296.80	12.30	126.78
2020	17581	43.69	225.61	8.93	86.63
2021	18370	45.33	232.53	7.92	112.99
2022	19739	41.52	166.07	7.40	80.95

III. Public Cultural Service

In 2022, China's cultural and tourism administrations made efforts to upgrade the public cultural service efficiency based on the *National Standards of Basic Public Services (2021)*. We conducted the 7th evaluation and classification of public libraries above township level, encouraged cultural centers and libraries to open branches, and explore new models of public cultural spaces in both urban and rural areas. The 2022 national and regional public cultural goods online procurement fairs were hosted. The review of innovation and development of 63 national public cultural service demonstration zones were carried out. 91 towns with recognition in their regions were identified as "home of folklore and traditional art". Volunteer service programs including the Spring Rain, and cultural service programs for elders, young people, and the disabled were further promoted. Innovative public cultural activities were organized, and the 19th Qunxing (Constellation) Award ceremony was successfully held, which gave awards to 30 productions and 18,000 performances of award-winning shows. We also organized 12,000 Chinese New Year galas in rural villages, with the visitor attendance number reaching 118 million. Efforts were made to promote the steady development of public tourism services, for instance, more toilets were built in tourist destinations, and the electronic map of toilets for tourists were put online. 96% of the toilets in destinations were pinpointed on mobile App. The national standards for evaluation the quality of toilets in tourist destinations were revised.

(1) Public Libraries[5]

By the end of the year, there were in total 3,303 libraries nationwide, 88 more than the number of the previous year. The total number of employees of public libraries across China reached 60,740, 1,439 more than the number of the previous year. Among them, 7,850 owned senior professional titles, accounting for 12.9%, and 19,103 owned medium-level professional titles, accounting for 31.5%.

According to statistics at the end of 2022, the actual floor space used by public library buildings totaled 20.98 million m^2, up by 9.6% over the end of the previous year. 1.35959 billion books[6] were collected in these libraries, up by 7.8%. The number of seats in reading rooms was 1.55 million, up by 15.4%.

By the end of the 2022, the floor space of public libraries for each ten thousand persons was 148.61 m^2, an increase of 13.1 m^2 over the end of the previous year; the number of books per capita was 0.96, an increase of 0.07 over the previous year; the money spent on books per capita was 1.67 yuan, a decrease of 0.1 yuan over previous year.

Figure 1: Information of per capita resource of national public libraries in 2012-2022

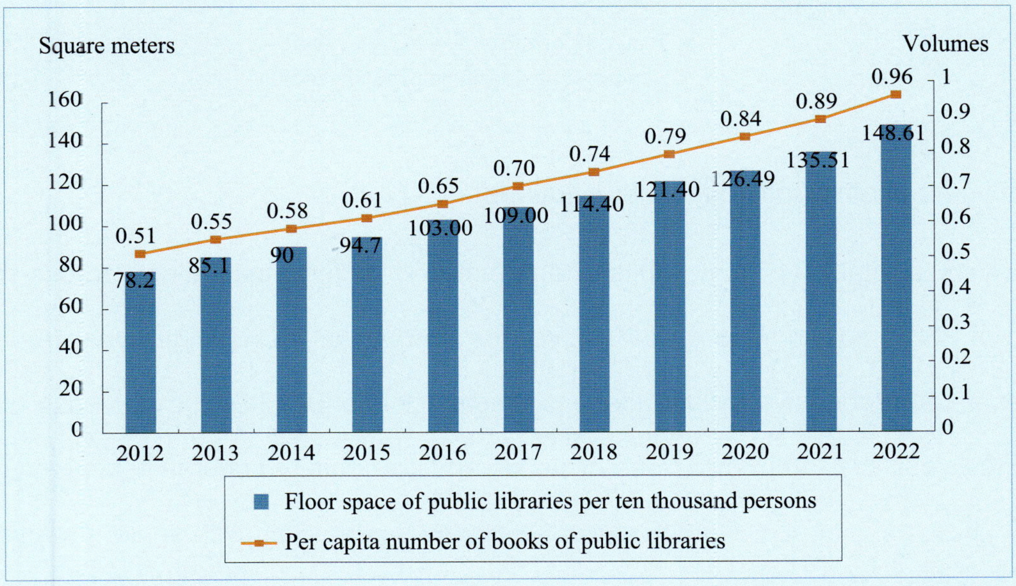

In 2022, public libraries across China issued 122.29 million library cards in total; the total flow of person-time in public libraries[7] reached 789.70 million, growing by 5.8%. The total circulation number of books, magazines, and documents loaned to readers reached 607.19 million, up by 3.4%; readers borrowed books for a total of 248.94 million times, 4.6% more than the number of previous year. The number of various activities organized for readers totaled 212,300, up by 4.8%, which attracted 134.95 million attendances, an increase of 13.5%. Further efforts were made to build smart library network across the country to deliver better service to readers through the internet and in libraries.

Figure 2: Total flow of person-time and number of books lent out of national public libraries in 2012-2022

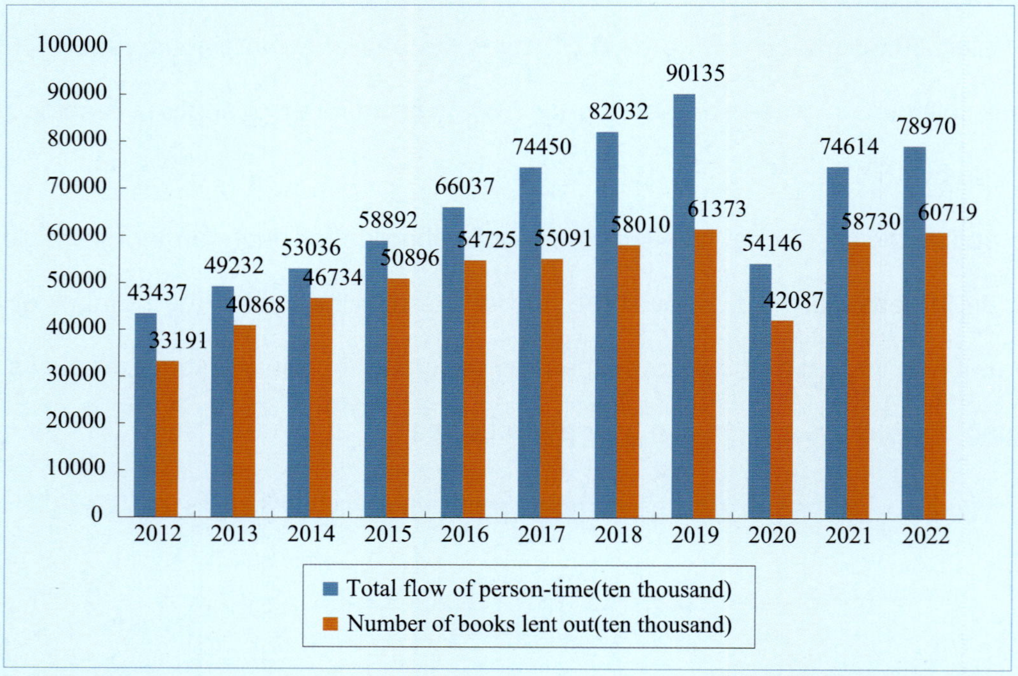

(2) Public and community cultural institutions[8]

There were a total of 45,623 public and community cultural institutions across the country by the end of 2022, an increase of 2,092 over the number of the previous year. Among these, township-level comprehensive cultural stations reached a total of 33,932, a decrease of 1 408. By the end of the year, the total employees of public and community cultural institutions nationwide reached 195,826, an increase of 5,819 since the previous year. Staff with senior professional titles reached 7,868, accounting for 4.0%; and staffs with medium-grade professional titles reached 18,262, accounting for 9.3%.

By the end of the year, the actual floor space used by public and community institutions was 52.98 million m^2, up by 6.5% since the previous year; among them, the floor space used for offering public services was 36.68 million m^2, up by 3.7%. By the end of the year, the area covered by cultural facilities for every ten thousand people reached 375.25 m^2, an increase of 6.6% since the previous year.

Figure 3: Area of structure of national cultural facilities of mass per ten thousand people in 2012-2022

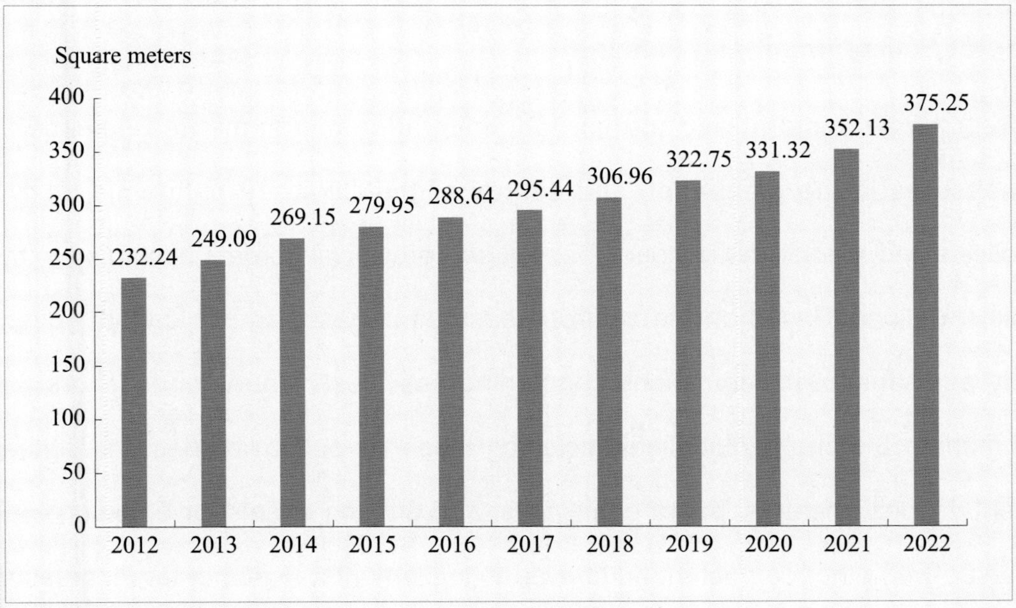

The number of activities[9] organized by nationwide public and community cultural institutions throughout the year reached 2.7073 million, up by 7.4% since the previous year; they provided services for 959.22 million times, up by 15.2%. They carried out in total 2.8096 million online public cultural activities throughout the year.

By the end of the year, public and community cultural institutions[10] nationwide fostered a total of 9,322 cultural and arts organizations under cultural centers, which presented 103,200 performances to a total audience of 54.42 million. The number of amateur cultural and arts organizations supported by cultural centers (stations) totaled to 463,600.

Table 2: Information of activities organized by nationwide public and community cultural institutions in 2022

	Gross		Increase over previous year (%)	
	Number of activity (time)	Number of participants (ten thousand person-time)	Number of activity	Person-time of participants
Aggregate of activities	**2707286**	**95922**	**7.4**	**15.2**
#Art Performances	1607329	68474	15.5	10.2
Workshops	879961	6811	-4.4	11.3
Exhibitions	177506	19872	6.0	39.4
Free Lectures	42490	762	1.3	-0.8

IV. Market Management and Policing

In 2022, China's cultural and tourism administrations implemented science-based and targeted measures in the prevention and control of the Covid-19 pandemic, and constantly adjusted policies and regulations for tours that crossed provincial borders according to the changes of pandemic situations. Based on the control measures released by the central government, we made timely adjustments to regulations concerning activities, venues and visitors, and revised in a timely manner 8 industry guidelines including those for public libraries and cultural centers, entertainment venues, theaters, board game bars, and grading exams for amateur-level art skills. We also worked with other competent authorities to implement a series of target measures to help the recovery of cultural and tourism sectors, such as tax and fee deduction, job vacancy guarantee and employment support, delayed payment of employees' social insurance, financial support and deduction of rent. We refunded 100% of domestic travel agencies' service quality deposits, and the total sum of refunded or deposits reached 9.6 billion yuan. We approved the pilot reform campaign of travel agencies' service quality deposits in 14 provinces and cities including Hainan, and hosted the cultural and tourism business service month, unrolling over 800 incentive activities and measures for companies.

The Ministry continued to improve the market and business environment, as we established a comprehensive list of administrative permits, further promoted the one-stop system for administrative affairs, allowed longer time for inconvenienced entities to complete necessary procedures, fully applied the rating system, and established the management system for electronic certificates and licenses in cultural and tourism markets. We revised 2 trade regulations and 30 administrative rules for performing arts agents, commercial shows, entertainment venues, B&B in rural areas and board game businesses. We published the guidelines for building capacity of travel agents and encouraging responsible tourism in destinations, issued the three-year training plan for star hotel staff, and completed the evaluation of level-A travel agents across the country. More regulations were implemented for livestreaming, commercial endorsements and vloggers. Measures were taken to guarantee the order of holiday travels including those in the periods of New Year, Chinese New Year, Labor Day holiday and National Day holiday, and safety of tourists in flood seasons and summer vacations.

By the end of the year, business units in the nationwide cultural market[11] reached 202,800, with 1.34 million employees, according to data submitted by these units. Throughout the year, their sales reached 1,410.644 billion yuan, with a profit of 234.997 billion yuan.

By the end of 2022, travel agencies across the country reached 32,603. According to the statistics of the travel agency database, their total sales in 2022 reached 160.156 billion yuan, with a loss of 6.887 billion yuan.

By the end of the year, there were in total 8,365 star hotels in China. Among them, the statistics of 7,337 were checked by cultural and tourism administrations. According to the statistics they report, their total sales in 2022 reached 117.768 billion yuan, with the average daily rate (ADR) of 318.48 yuan room/night and the average occupancy rate of 38.35%.

In 2022, the Ministry's comprehensive policing system for the cultural market were further improved. We issued uniforms and badges for over 30,000 officers and improved their certification and badge system. 29 provinces, regions and cities published the guidelines of items that needs policing, and 20 provinces, regions and cities drafted the standards for the discretion of administrative penalties. Actions to guarantee the strong policing of cultural and tourism market on the eve of the 20th CPC national congress was taken, and efforts were made to strengthen policing supervision during the Beijing Winter Olympics. We also made solid progresses in regulating cultural and entertainment sectors, banned cultural productions involving artists who failed to comply with the "self-discipline" guideline, and carried out the special operation to regulate the artwork market. Constant efforts were made to combat cross-border gambling with the facade of tourism, as well as to put a stop to the business of travel agencies with no appropriate license and the hoax budget travel packages. We conducted three rounds of unannounced checks and evaluations on over 1,200 companies in 29 provinces, regions and cities. Online monitoring was normalized, and we checked on over 54,000 tips. Hotlines of cultural and tourism markets were integrated, and 31,000 complaints were dealt with. Throughout the year, 9.31 million dispatches were made to police the cultural and tourism market across the country, during which 3,3[illegible] million checks on business properties were made, and over 36,000 cases were closed. On-site and online training programs with case studies and lectures were organized, offering 13,000 training opportunities.

V. Resource Development

In 2022, the Ministry formulated the plan to build the Yangtze River national cultural park and conserve its environment, drafted and implemented plans to build Beijing-Zhangjiakou sports and cultural tourism belt, Sichuan culture and tourism corridor, and Hangzhou-Huangshan natural and cultural corridor tourism corridor. We improved the plans to build world-lass tourism destinations and resorts, issued the new national standards for the classification of resorts, published the *Outline for Tourism and Leisure Development of the Chinese People (2022-2030)*, and released the guiding opinions of 14 ministries and departments on leisure camping. Efforts were made to provide more travel products. 23 provinces, regions and cities carried out tourism resource census, and we newly certified 12 national-level 5A destinations, 15 national-level resorts, 54 national-level tourism and leisure streets, 53 national-level industry tourism demonstration zones, 12 national-level ski resorts, and 14 demonstration destinations for sports tourism. Efforts were made to upgrade rural tourism, as we announced the fourth national-level list of key villages (498 villages in total) specialized in rural tourism, and recommended 369 travel routes for tourists to discover the the charm of different villages in different seasons, and 8 routes to enjoy the Great Wall. Dazhai village in Guangxi autonomous region and Jinzhu village in Chongqing municipality were named among the best tourism villages by the UNWTO. Innovative promotions were made to advertise China's tourism, as we co-produced CCTV programs that introduced the nature and culture of China. Domestic tourism promotions were also made, including the Beautiful China, Better Life events, and various special programs to feature different cities in different seasons. The second national tourism public interest advertisement selection and presentation program was organized. We published the guidelines for smart tourism scenarios (trial), and carried out the program to use cloud and digital technology to make tourism smarter. We started to explore the integration of revolutionary heritage and tourism. We organized red tourism (tourism to sites of significance in early CPC history) package planning competition for college students as well as the lectures of tour guides in red tourism sites on campus, presenting over 11,000 events with 47 million attendances of college, middle school and primary school students.

By the end of this year, there were 14,917 A-level tourist sites in China, with 1.47 million employees. Their total revenue in 2022 reached 181.85 billion yuan, with total visits of 2.63 billion.

Throughout the year, 2.53 billion domestic visits were made by Chinese tourists, decreasing by 22.1% over that of the previous year. The revenue of domestic tourism (total tourism expenditure) totaled 2.04 trillion yuan, down by 30.0% over that of the previous year.

Figure 4: Domestic tourism developinent in 2012-2022

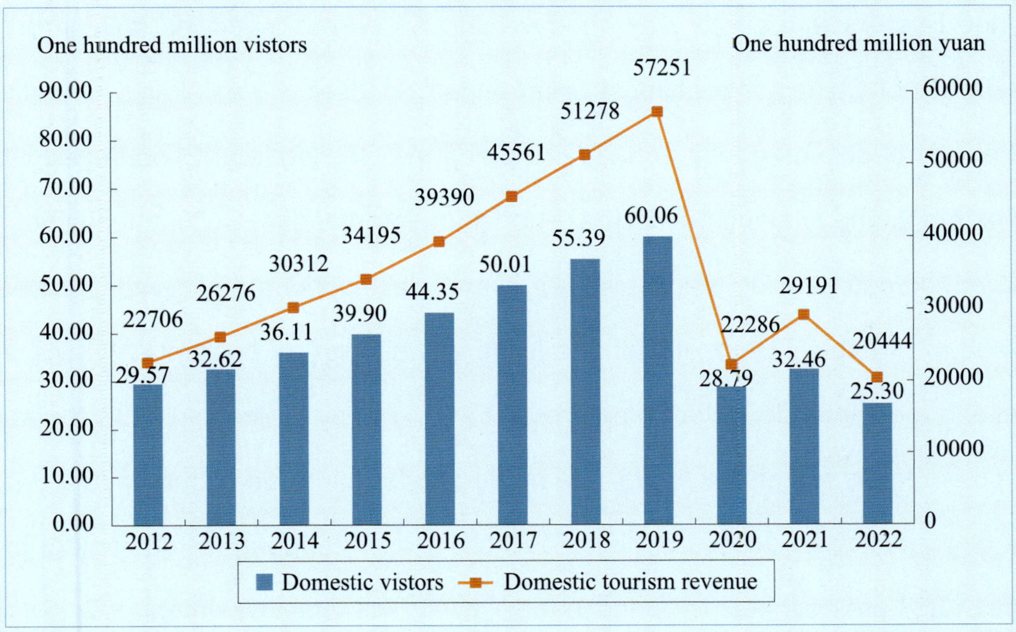

VI. Cultural and Tourism Industries and Related Technology

In 2022, the Ministry published the opinions on promoting rural revitalization through cultural industry, and started the pilot programs to reach this goal. We implemented the plan to integrate the development of cultural industry parks into the overall advancement of cultural industry in that region. We published the second list of 123 best nightlife zones nationwide, and executed the program to stimulate spending on culture and tourism in a hundred cities and districts for the benefit of business growth and the increase of people's income. We also supported the rapid development of digital culture, and encouraged the use of technologies such as 5G and UHD. We urged state-owned art companies to develop programs such as the online broadcasting of performing arts productions during the War of Resistance against Japan, and the digital copy of dance drama Unfading Green. Together with other institutions, we published an action plan on integrating VR technology into the development of cultural industry to support new forms of business such as online video broadcasting and immersive experience showcases. We joined the Ministry of Commerce to publish a notice on a new round of application of national-level bases for international cultural trade and based related work on this document. In Jingdezhen, Jiangxi Province, we hosted a special cultural and tourism trade promotion event with the focus on porcelain. Together with the Ministry of Economy, Trade and Industry of Japan and the Ministry of Culture, Sports and Tourism of the Republic of Korea, we hosted the 15th China-Japan-ROK Cultural Industry Forum, and supported East Asian e-sports exchange events. We co-published the opinion on supporting the quality growth of China's international cultural trade, revised the catalogue of statistics on the import and export of cultural goods and services, and the Catalogue of Encouraged Industries for Foreign Investment, and held the 18th China (Shenzhen) International Cultural Industries Fair. While we established the coordination mechanism for overall development of different business projects, we also joined the People's Bank of China to issue a "white list" of backbone cultural and tourism enterprises, and recommended over 30 enterprises and 171 key projects to apply for policy-backed and development loans for infrastructure. We made efforts to include cultural and tourism projects into the list of projects with access to policy-backed, discounted loan for equipment procurement and upgrade. 1,237 projects were included in the list, with the total investment of 24.61 billion yuan.

We also completed the work to nominate 10 cities and regions to be included in the 2021 list of the General Office of the State Council of China to enjoy incentives for the development of cultural and travel industries.

According to the National Bureau of Statistics, in 2022, the total turnover of major cultural and culture related businesses reached 12180.5 billion yuan, increasing by 0.9% over that of the previous year. Among them, the turnover of 16 sectors booming with new business forms reached 4386 billion yuan, increasing by 5.3%.

In 2022, the Ministry advanced the implementation of the national strategy of digitizing cultural properties, recognized 12 national-level demonstration zones and parks for tourism-related technology, and gave financial support to 14 key laboratories under the Ministry to implement the key national-level R&D programs in cultural and tourism fields. We announced three practices to be the best innovative practices in cultural and tourism fields, namely the Tang dynasty cultural presentations featuring A Day in Changan and Datang Everbright City, the “readable architecture” in Shanghai, and the dance drama Unfading Green. We co-published the opinion on promoting the quality development of standards for associations, and made contributions to the release of 4 national standards, including those for stage facilities, toilets in tourist destinations, resorts and B&B hotels, and nominated 1 standard for evaluation. We published 7 trade standards including those for safety in performing arts shows and services of group leader in outbound travels, and nominated 30 for evaluation. We also proposed 18 major projects, 219 annual projects and 51 ministerial social science research projects in the field of art studies to apply for the National Social Science Fund of China. 36 projects were carried out under the umbrella of 2022 supporting program for young researchers in the cultural and tourism administrations. The Ministry also made further efforts to build think tanks for cultural and tourism sectors, and advanced our work to cooperate with universities. We published the guiding opinion on the promotion of quality development of vocational education in the fields of culture and arts in the new era, and identified 115 projects to be included in the action plan to improve culture, arts and tourism vocational education across the country. We held the 7th graduate program for young Peking opera artists, which enrolled 54 students, and the capacity building (undergraduate) program for local cultural talents in Tibet and Xinjiang, which enrolled 24 students.

VII. Cultural Heritage Conservation and Management

In 2022, the Ministry further improved its top-tier design for heritage work, as we held a high-level national working conference on cultural heritage to identify the principles of cultural heritage work in the new era as stronger protection, better management, and responsible exploration of potential and value to make heritage viable and sustainable. Thanks to the efforts of the Ministry, the opinion on strengthen the international standing of Chinese culture by bringing cultural heritage to life was ready for release, the regulation on the preservation and management of underwater cultural heritage was revised, the the special plan for archaeological work in the 14th Five-Year-Plan period was published. The project aimed at tracing the origins of Chinese civilization made new breakthroughs. We pushed ahead the key archaeological projects of China including the ones focusing on Xia culture and Koguryo, and released 17 important achievements made in such areas as paleolithic archaeology, the origin of the human race, the Yin ruins, and oracle inscription bones. Heritage conservation in urban infrastructure development was given more importance, as 23 provinces and cities have implemented the policy of conducting archaeological research before land transfer. We pool resources to build the archaeological species archive in key heritage sites, implemented the national capacity building program for archaeologists, released the fourth list of national heritage site park, and did related work to make sure monument management be included in the outline of national plan for territorial development. Thanks to our efforts to normalize the tracing and repatriation of cultural relics, 29 cultural relics returned to China. We initiated the digital restoration program of looted Chinese relics overseas, and completed the project to preserve and valorize revolutionary heritage (2018-2022), as 16 provinces reviewed and published the second list of revolutionary heritage items. To bring new life to cultural heritage, we hosted several events including the heritage-theme promotion on the 2022 cultural and natural heritage day, and the celebration of international museum day in China.We published the opinions on encouraging and supporting the private sector to contribute to the conservation and management of historical buildings. TV shows we co-produced, such as Chinese Archaeology Assembly and Chinese

National Treasure Assembly, were widely acclaimed.

By the end of the year, there were 11,340 cultural heritage institutions all over China, an increase of 795 over the number of the previous year. Among these, 2,663 were for the preservation of cultural relics, accounting for 23.5%; and 3,782 were state-owned museums[12] managed by heritage administrations, accounting for 33.4%. By the end of the year, the number of employees by cultural heritage institutions reached 190,300, an increase of 8,800 compared to the end of the previous year. Among them, 12,757 were with senior professional titles, accounting for 6.7%; and 24,129 were with medium-grade professional titles, accounting for 12.7%.

Figure 5: Information of national cultural relics agencies and employed persons in 2012-2022

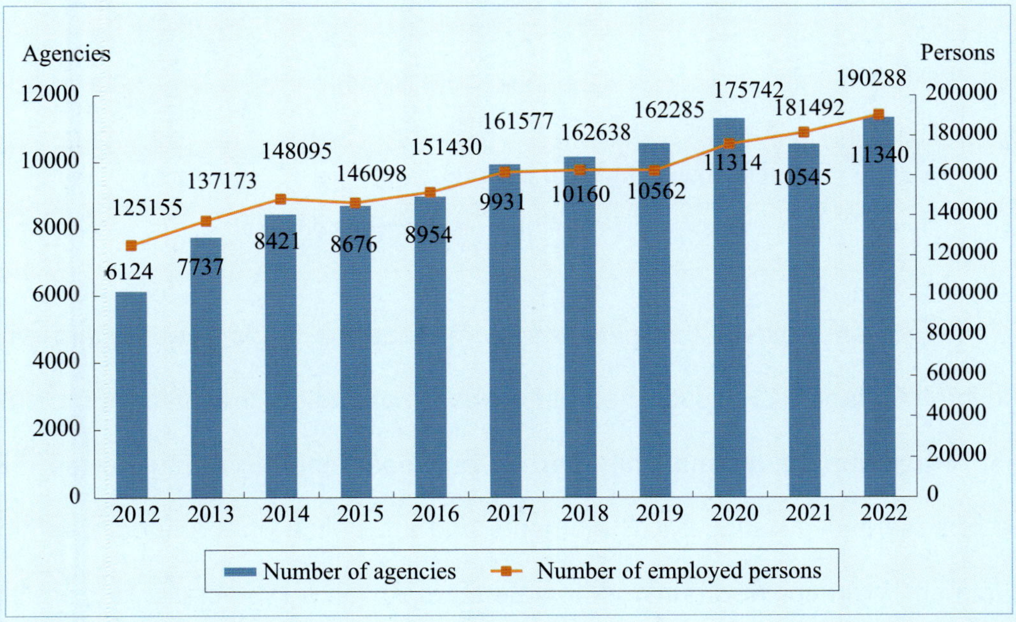

By the end of the year, there were 56.3043 million items of collections of cultural relics in the cultural heritage institutions. Among these, the amount of collections in museums totaled to 46.9161 million, which accounted for 83.3% of the total.

In 2022, 32,357 exhibitions were displayed across the country, 848 less than those of the previous year. Throughout the year, the number of nationwide basic exhibitions[13] arranged by cultural heritage institutions reached 17,399, decreased by 198 over that of the previous year; and temporary exhibitions[14] totaled 14,958, down by 650; the number of visitor attendances reached

639.73 million, which was a decrease of 24.4% over that of the previous year. Among these, 456.47 million visits were to state-owned museums managed by heritage administrations, down by 22.8%. Among the visitors, the number of minors was 160.04 million, down by 16.9%, accounting for 25.0% of all visitors.

Figure 6: Person-time of audiences and minors cultural relic agencies accepting in 2012-2022

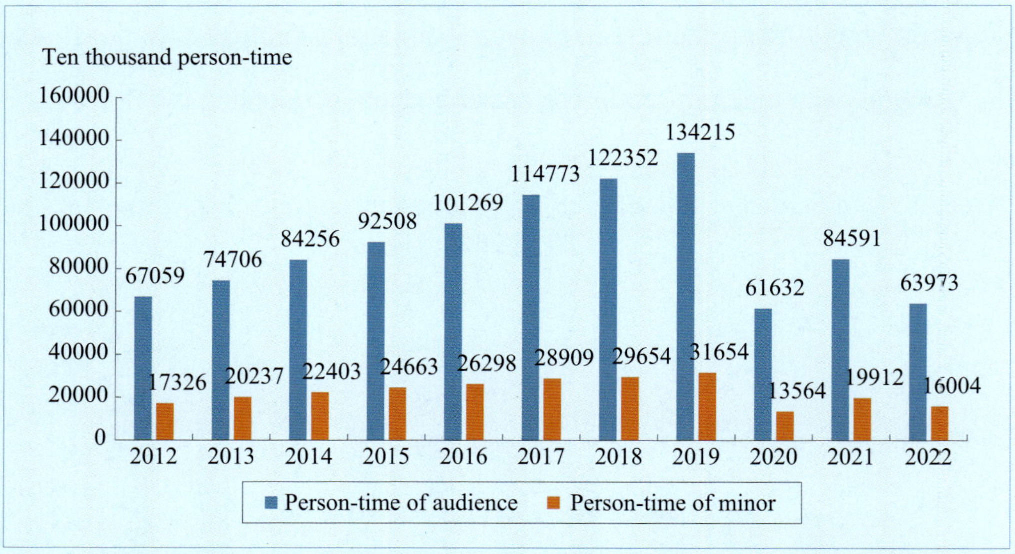

In 2022, the Ministry revised the measures to manage the funds to safeguard national-level intangible cultural heritage (ICH), published the notice on promoting the effective transmission and development of traditional craftsmanship, carried out researches to formulate the measures to manage the representative national ICH elements and the notice on the integrated development of ICH and tourism. We improved our work to safeguard ICH in a systematic way, and made great efforts to ensure that traditional tea processing techniques and their associated social practices in China were added to UNESCO's Representative List of the Intangible Cultural Heritage of Humanity. We initiated the work to appraise national ICH bearers and conducted the acceptance check of the national-level cultural heritage reserves, continued to carry out the pilot programs of safeguarding ICH in communities, further implemented the traditional craftsmanship revitalization plan, the quyi opera transmission and development plan and the ICH bearer capacity building program, and initiated the nomination of national-level demonstration zones for keeping ICH viable by exploring their commodity values. We advanced the work to develop ICH studies discipline, and made great efforts to raise public awareness on ICH, as over 6,200 activities held across the country to celebrate ICH, including the ICH-theme event on 2022 cultural and natural heritage day, the photo and video exhibition of ICH, ICH shopping festival, the 7th China ICH Expo, the ICH exhibition with the focus on Xinjiang Autonomous Region and 19 provinces and cities which offered paired assistance to Xinjiang, the campaign to encourage creators to promote Chinese New Year traditions and folklore through vlogging and live broadcasting at several websites, and the Tea for Harmony: ICH for Share program. We also joined China Media Group to co-produce a TV program named China in ICH. More than 2,500 ICH workshops were build across the country, including those in over 450 counties that just emerged from poverty and 85 key counties to receive assistance in pursuing rural revitalization.

By the end of 2022, there were 2,433 national-level representative intangible cultural heritage (ICH) bearers recognized by the Ministry of Culture and Tourism who were still alive and 1,557 national-level representative ICH elements endorsed by the State Council. There were 43 Chinese elements inscribed on the UNESCO Representative List of the Intangible Cultural Heritage of Humanity, more than any other countries in the world.

By the end of 2022, there were a total of 2,425 ICH safeguarding institutions across the country, with 17,716 employees. Throughout the year in the country, these institutions held 57,762 showcases, down by 3.3%, 13,664 folklore activities, up by 4.2%, and 18,107 exhibitions, same as that of the previous year.

VIII. International Cultural and Tourism Exchange and Bonding with Hong Kong, Macao and Taiwan Regions

In 2022, with a focus on carrying out the central task and serving the overall interests of the country, the Ministry significantly contributed to the success of Beijing Winter Olympics and Paralympics, hosted the welcome gala for international VIP guests of the Olympics, the Happy Chinese New Year temple fair, Meet in Beijing international arts festival and Olympics cultural festival, and the promotion event of ice and snow tourism season. We promoted several routes of ice and snow tourism in China and national ski resorts with well-curated cultural activities.

We implemented the three-year action plan of Silkroad of Culture, and supported the World Tourism Association to put its headquarters in Hangzhou. We also hosted events including the China International Travel Mark, Discover China, and East Asia Capital of Culture, and co-hosted the global tour of China Documentary Festival, China Tourism and Culture Week overseas, and the exhibition of ICH's role in poverty reduction. The Ministry organized the 2022 Happy Chinese New Year events, and designed and presented 14 online cultural and tourism programs in three categories, namely traditional culture, ice and snow, and Chinese lifestyle, which attracted over 626.1 million views of international audience.

The Ministry hosted the China-Russia cultural and tourism ministers' meeting, and such events as the China-Russia Cultural Fair. We attended the Edinburgh international cultural summit and the 59th Venice Biennale, as well as participated in such cooperation mechanisms as ASEAN-China-Japan-ROK, China-ASEAN and China-Japan-ROK by holding meetings of cultural and tourism ministers. We implemented the Asian Tourism Promotion Plan, organized anniversary celebrations of diplomatic ties with 12 Asian, African and Latin American countries including Argentina, participated the 14th Dakar Biennale of Contemporary African Art and the 14th Havana Biennial, organized capacity building workshops for African countries, hosted the BRICS cultural minister's meeting and tourism ministers' meeting, and attended the 2022 UNWTO World Conference on Tourism Cooperation and Development.

With the aim to nurture the root and identity of the nation, the Ministry of Culture and Tourism continued to deepen cultural and tourism bonding with Hong Kong, Macao and Taiwan. We held the opening ceremony of Hong Kong Palace Museum, supported Hong Kong to host the Asia Cultural Co-operation Forum 2022, and unrolled a series of cultural heritage events to celebrate the 25th anniversary of Hong Kong's return to the motherland. We also supported Macao to host the China (Macao) Creative Industry Conference and the Macao International Travel (Industry) Expo, and helped 18 projects from Hong Kong and Macao to successfully land the funding of National Arts Fund of China. We hosted the field trip for Taiwan visitors to Qinghai, and the ICH month engaging both Chinese mainland and Taiwan. We participated in the tourism exhibitions in Taipei and Gaoxiong, and organized such activities as the cultural experience trips for college students from Hong Kong and Macao, virtual trips for young people from Hong Kong and Macao to Chinese mainland, and cultural and tourism exchange event between young people from both sides of the Taiwan strait.

By the end of the year, there were in total 45 overseas China Cultural Centers and 20 Chinese tourism offices in foreign countries. Moreover, we also have established the Asia Tourism Exchange Center in Hong Kong, and the offices of Association For Tourism Exchange Across The Taiwan Straits in Taipei and Gaoxiong.

IX. Budget

In 2022, steady progresses were made in the development of major cultural projects, including the completion of the China Arts and Crafts Museum (CTCM) and the new theater of China National Opera House. The projects to restore the north compound of the Palace Museum and to build new halls of the National Ballet of China were initiated. The project to preserve and transmit traditional culture during the 14th Five-Year-Plan advanced smoothly.

Figure 7: National cultural and tourism undertaking expenses per capita (2012-2022)

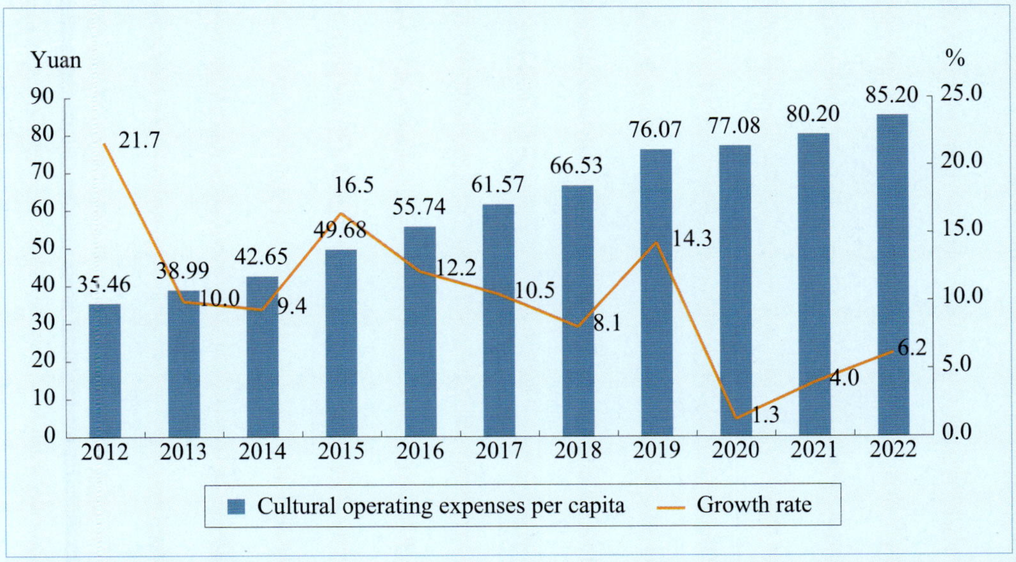

The total amount of cultural and tourism undertaking expenses[15] for the whole year was 120.289 billion yuan, an increase of 7.001 billion yuan over that of the previous year, up by 6.2%;

as for the national cultural and tourism undertaking expenses per capita, the total was 85.20 yuan, an increase of 5 yuan over the previous year, up by 6.2%. Cultural and tourism undertaking expenses accounted for 0.46% of the state expenditure of China, basically the same with that of the previous year.

Table 3: Urban & Rural and Regional-based distribution of national cultural undertaking expenses

		In 1995	In 2000	In 2005	In 2010	In 2015	In 2020	In 2021	In 2022
Aggregate (one hundred million yuan)	**Nationwide**	**33.4**	**63.2**	**133.8**	**323.1**	**686.0**	**1088.3**	**1132.9**	**1202.9**
	# Above county level	24.4	46.3	98.1	206.7	352.8	501.0	506.4	544.3
	County level and below level of county	9.0	16.9	35.7	116.4	330.1	587.3	626.5	658.6
	# Eastern region	13.4	28.9	64.4	143.4	287.9	491.6	526.4	542.5
	Central region	9.5	15.1	30.6	78.7	164.3	269.8	283.4	302.6
	Western region	8.3	13.7	27.6	85.8	193.9	301.6	292.6	328.1
Proportion (%)	**Nationwide**	**100**	**100**	**100**	**100**	**100**	**100**	**100**	**100**
	# Above county level	73.2	73.4	73.3	64.0	51.7	46.0	44.7	45.2
	County level and below level of county	26.8	26.7	26.7	36.0	48.3	54.0	55.3	54.8
	# Eastern region	40.2	45.7	48.1	44.4	42.1	45.1	46.5	45.1
	Central region	28.6	23.8	22.9	24.3	24.1	24.8	25.0	25.2
	Western region	24.9	21.7	20.6	26.6	28.4	27.7	25.3	27.3

Regarding the national cultural and tourism undertaking expenses, that of cultural and tourism units above county level was 54.429 billion yuan, accounting for 45.2%, 0.5 percentage points higher than that of the previous year; that of cultural and tourism units of county level or below the level of county was 65.861 billion yuan, accounting for 54.8%, down by 1.4 percentage points in the sense of its proportion. The cultural and tourism undertaking expenses of eastern region[16] reached 54.253 billion yuan, accounting for 45.1%, and its proportion decreased by 1.4%; that of central region reached 30.256 billion yuan, accounting for 25.2%, its proportion increased by 0.2%; and that of western region reached 32.809 billion yuan, accounting for 27.3%, 1.5 percentage points lower than the number of the previous year.

Notes:

[1] All the data of the communiqué are preliminary statistical data. HKSAR, MSAR, and Taiwan Province are not included in each data. Some of data are not compatible with the total of subentries due to rounding off.

[2] Cultural and tourism units refers to cultural institutions that national cultural and tourism departments of all levels organize or implement industrial management, excluding cultural institutions organized or managed by the departments of all levels of press and publications, radio , film and television, etc. According to the current statistical system, the cultural institutions (such as public libraries, cultural centers, cultural stations, museums, etc.) organized by cultural departments are brought into the statistical range. Regarding cultural institutions with industrial management, the private art performance troupes, cybercafé, and entertainment venues are brought into statistical range, while the mechanism of exchange of works of art, internet culture institution are not in the range.

[3] The employees refer to the people who work and receive working rewards in the institutions that cultural and tourism departments at all levels organize or implement industrial management.

[4] The art performance troupes mean various professional artistic performance organizations which are organized by cultural and tourism institutions or to which the cultural institutions implement industrial management (with approval of cultural administration department and commercial performance license), and is engaged in such activities as performing arts.

[5] Public library refers to all kinds of institutions that are organized by cultural departments at all levels, and is open to public as well as providing popularization and education of science,

culture, and other knowledge.

[6] The total collection of books in public libraries refers to the sum of audiovisual literature materials including bound volume, manual, manuscript, micro-reproduction, videotape, audio tape and CD of ancient books, books, periodicals and newspapers in catalogue. It does not include digital books.

[7] The total flow of person-time in public library refers to the gross person-time of receiving the service of the libraries in that year, including borrowing books, consultation and participating in various readers' activities.

[8] The mass cultural institutions refer to the places that cultural departments at all levels organize for mass cultural activities, mainly including cultural centers (including comprehensive cultural center and mass art gallery) and cultural stations.

[9] That the mass cultural institution organizes and carries out activities means the sum of the organizations of cultural literary and artistic activities, training classes, exhibitions, and public lectures.

[10] The literature and art organizations of mass cultural institutions refer to performance teams composed by the staff of this institution and that provide performances for the mass.

[11] The operating units of cultural markets refer to the agencies which are approved or filed by administrative departments of cultural markets and have relevant licenses and filing documents, and that engage in cultural management and services. In line with the current statistical systems, the statistical range of operating units of the cultural market only include private art performance troupes, entertainment venues, and business sites of internet access services.

[12] The museum refers to the non-profit and permanent social service institution which collects, preserves, and exhibits the witness of human activity and natural environment with intent of research, education, and appreciation, as well as being open to the public. It includes the units that carry out activities with proper names such as museums, memorial halls, science and technology museums, exhibition halls, etc.

[13] Basic exhibition refers to the exhibition which is displayed in the pavilion, with fixed location and for an extended time.

[14] Temporary exhibition means the multi-formed exhibition which is set in the institution and designed by the pavilion.

[15] Cultural operating expense means aggregate of expenditures that the finance of all levels in the area invests to the organizer of cultural systems. It generally includes financial appropriation (excluding appropriations of capital construction costs) of cultural institutions such as art performance troupes, public libraries, cultural centers (stations), etc. and financial subsidies of enterprises subordinate to the Ministry of Culture. According to current statistical caliber, cultural operating expense does not include administrative operation expenditures of cultural administration and management departments at all levels.

[16] Eastern region includes Beijing, Tianjin, Liaoning Province, Shanghai, Jiangsu Province, Fujian Province, Shandong Province, and Guangdong Province; Central region includes Hebei Province, Shanxi Province, Jilin Province, Heilongjiang Province, Anhui Province, Jiangxi Province, Henan Province, Hubei Province, Hunan Province and Hainan Province; Western region includes Inner Mongolia (autonomous region), Guangxi Province, Chongqing, Sichuan Province, Guizhou Province, Yunan Province, Tibet (autonomous region), Shaanxi Province, Gansu Province, Qinghai Province, Ningxia (autonomous region), and Xinjiang (autonomous region).